RHUM
Klapholz

By Deirdre Stanforth

THE NEW ORLEANS RESTAURANT COOKBOOK

Creole!

THE LEGENDARY CUISINE OF NEW ORLEANS:

GUMBO, JAMBALAYA, GRILLADES, FRICASSEE; THE GREAT

SEAFOOD SPECIALTIES, THE MOST OPULENT SWEETS.

55 AUTHENTIC RECIPES

PLUS FASCINATING LORE FOR THE COOK.

Deirdre Stanforth

Decorations by Mel Klapholz

SIMON AND SCHUSTER · NEW YORK

Published by Simon and Schuster
Rockefeller Center, 630 Fifth Avenue
New York, New York 10020

First printing

SBN 671-20354-1
Library of Congress Catalog Card Number: 78-84133
Designed by Edith Fowler
Manufactured in the United States of America

To Tess Crager
with love

Contents

Introduction

What Is Creole Cuisine? 10, What Is a Roux? 12, Rice 13, Some Helpful Hints 14

I. Soups

Avery Island Creamed Onion Soup 19, Cream of Crab Soup 20, Oyster Soup 21

II. Gumbos

Seafood Gumbo Filé 25, Okra-Seafood Gumbo 26, Chicken Gumbo 28

III. Eggs

Absinthe Baked Eggs 31, Creole Omelet 32, Eggs Soufflé au Gratin 33, Fish Soufflé 34, Sauce for Fish Soufflé 35, Crab Soufflé 36

IV. Seafood Specialties

Oysters with Mushrooms 39, Oysters in Red Wine 40, Oyster Loaf 41, Artichokes and Oysters 42, Creole Stuffed Cabbage 44,

Crabmeat Lafayette 46, Crabmeat with Mushrooms 48, Stuffed Crabs 49, Seafood Mardi Gras 50, Broiled Shrimp 51, Shrimp and Crab Fricassee 52, Cold Redfish Mayonnaise 54, Sauce Tartare 55

V. Rice Dishes

Creole Jambalaya 59, Ham Jambalaya 60, Hopping John 61, Red Beans and Rice I 62, Red Beans and Rice II 63, Shrimp Creole 64, Grillades 65, Chicken Fricassee Pointe Coupée 66, Creole Courtbouillon 68

VI. Vegetables

Creole String Beans 71, Stewed Okra and Tomatoes 72, Lettuce au Jus 73, Baked Cabbage au Gratin 74, Baked Celery 75, Spinach and Asparagus 76, Fried Eggplant 77, Stuffed Eggplant 78, Stuffed Peppers 79, Julius Caesar Tomatoes 80

VII. Accompaniments

Confederate Pudding (Baked Grits) 83, Corn Bread Dressing 84, Oyster-Mushroom Gravy 85, Fried Grits 86, Sweet Potato Balls 87

VIII. Sweets

Frozen Buttermilk 91, Brandy Custard 92, Rum Bananas 93, Plum-Pecan Conserve 94, Pralines 95

Introduction

Creole cooking is the only cuisine of any consequence to have originated in America. It is derivative of numerous native elements: French, Spanish, Italian, American Indian and Negro, but the sum total results in a cooking style different from any other—piquant and delicious. For many years there has been a general misconception of the meaning of the word Creole. It has nothing to do with mulatto; it refers to one born in the southern colonies of parents native to other lands—usually French, Spanish or both. This definition is equally applicable to Creole cuisine—you might say it has taken the finest attributes of the cooking of these nationalities, mixed well, and produced a very special style unlike any of its origins. It is strange that until recently this unique and important American cuisine has been so generally unknown and neglected in the country at large. This is beginning to change, and I hope this book will help it to attain the popularity it so obviously deserves.

The recipes presented here came from private collections of New Orleans and New Iberia, Louisiana; some have been passed down through families, others are newer variations on the Creole theme; many have never been published before. The generosity and graciousness of many people has made this collection possible. New Orleanians, notably Connie Kaufman, Irma Rosen, Ray Freeman and Glen Douthit, among others, were most helpful, and I am particularly proud to be able to pass on the very special and delightful recipes of Mrs. Lou McLaughlin, a great lady of the great Avery-McIlhenny family of Avery Island. I was also extremely fortunate to have as a source the personal "receipt" collection of the late Mrs. Walter Torian, whose name is well known to New Orleans gourmets. This treasure was given to me by her nephew, the late Weeks Hall, a widely famed gentleman who lovingly preserved his family heritage in the fabulous New Iberia plantation "The Shadows on the Teche" (now a National Trust). I use the word "treasure" quite literally because Creoles have always been notoriously jealous of their recipes. Indeed, it was Mrs. Torian who, having sworn her devoted cook, Celimene, to secrecy, could not persuade her to divulge a favorite "receipt" even to herself when she had lost it.

What Is Creole Cuisine?

Creole cuisine seems to separate into two distinct categories: the more elegant dishes, which are spicier variations of French cooking, and the very different poor-folks or "soul" food, which depends more on its Negro-Indian ancestry. Climate and geography play an important part in the nature of Creole cuisine too: the fact that it was developed in New Orleans and environs, where seafood is plentiful, dictates that meat is seldom a featured ingredient: and the unfailing preference in tropical lands for hot spicy foods is a major factor in the total effect of Creole cooking.

Creole cuisine has a certain number of salient characteristics: a heavy dependency on rice, extensive use of tomatoes, green peppers and green onions (locally called bell peppers and shallots) in sauces; of thyme and bay leaf in seasoning; and the beginning of most recipes with a "roux" (see below). Filé powder, certainly a purely Creole spice, was originally made by the Choctaw Indians from sassafras leaves. Used in gumbos that do not include okra to impart the unique flavor and consistency, it is, oddly enough, widely available nationally in specialty food shops. (Note that filé is never cooked, or it becomes stringy. It is always stirred into a dish at the end, after it has been taken off the fire.)

In this book, seasoning is left to the discretion of the cook because it is very much a question of individual taste, but authentic Creole food is always highly seasoned and *very* hot! It was undoubtedly for this reason that the inimitable Louisiana hot sauce, Tabasco, was invented, and has become as basic an ingredient as any mentioned above.

Many of these recipes are absurdly easy and many are inexpensive, since they don't include prime cuts of meat. In fact, Red Beans and Rice makes as good a meal and is easier and cheaper to prepare than even the ubiquitous spaghetti and meatballs. Jambalaya (which is said to mean "clean up the kitchen") can be whipped up with all sorts of leftover odds and ends, and so can gumbo. Any of these dishes, with a salad and corn bread or French bread, makes a hearty meal for a crowd, earning compliments for the chef.

What Is a Roux?

A roux is simply the reverse of the usual American method of making gravy; rather than adding the flour or thickening agent to the juices at the end of the cooking, when it is likely to form lumps, it is mixed in at the beginning, just as flour is blended into the butter in making a cream sauce. So, in the beginning of most Creole dishes, you make a roux, melting fat, blending in an equal amount of flour (sometimes cooking until brown, sometimes not), then gradually stirring in liquid to make the sauce on which the dish is based.

Rice

Creole cuisine is so dependent on rice that it is absolutely essential to be able to produce dry, fluffy rice. Many people now prefer to use the virtually foolproof precooked rice, which comes with its own instructions. For those who like natural old-fashioned rice, here is the simplest and most widely used Creole method (there are many others).

To make rice: Fill a medium-to-large pot with salted water to within an inch or so of the top. As in cooking pasta, it is not necessary to measure the amount of water, or watch the clock. Bring water to a rolling boil and pour in the rice (about ¼ to ⅓ cup per serving). When it comes to a boil again, turn down so it continues to boil, but won't boil over. When rice is tender (about 15–20 minutes) pour contents of pot through a colander into the sink. Run hot water liberally through rice in the colander to wash off starchy residue. Put an inch or two of water in the same pot, set the colander full of rice on top and return to the stove. Bring to a boil and let steam 10–15 minutes, or until rice is well dried out and separated. Rice can be left steaming for a half hour or so if you are not ready to use it, but if it remains too long you will find some grains around the edges beginning to get hard and unusable. If you must keep rice steaming past a half hour (as when company is late for dinner) it is best to cover the colander loosely. You will find that this method easily produces dry, fluffy rice every time.

Some Helpful Hints

Since bacon fat is widely used in Creole cooking, imparting more flavor than other fats, it is a good idea always to pour leftover bacon fat into a coffee can with a plastic lid (or any can covered with foil) and keep it in the refrigerator. It can be stored there virtually indefinitely, constantly on hand to use in a roux.

It is also a good idea to make stock from any leftover bones and keep it in the freezer to enhance soups and sauces.

I have found that parsley to be used for seasoning freezes very well. You can cut off the stems and keep the whole bunch frozen in a plastic bag, simply cutting off the amount you need and returning the balance to the freezer. It is easier to chop than fresh parsley, thaws out instantly, is always available when you need it, and never has to be thrown away.

Some dishes, such as Shrimp Creole and Grillades, can be cooked in advance and reheated, often even improving in consistency and flavor; generally most baked dishes can be prepared a day or so ahead and kept in the refrigerator prior to baking and serving. Where freezing or storing is particularly applicable, this will be specified in the individual recipes.

In order to help Creole cuisine achieve the popularity it deserves, I have deliberately omitted dishes, no matter how famous or delicious, that require ingredients not generally available (such as crawfish), or that take all day to prepare. Although there are only half a hundred recipes in this little book, you can make a reputation as a superior cook with these alone—in fact I think you will find, as I have, that you can feed your family and friends with great ease and enormous success.

Soups

AVERY ISLAND CREAMED ONION SOUP

6 large onions, coarsely chopped
1½ quarts chicken stock
3 tablespoons butter
1 teaspoon sugar
6 tablespoons flour
1½ pints light cream
1 teaspoon salt, or to taste
dash Tabasco
2 ounces absinthe (Pernod) (optional)

In a soup pot boil 4 of the chopped onions in chicken stock 20–30 minutes. Sauté remaining chopped onions in butter until transparent. Sprinkle with sugar and blend in flour, then add to stock. Add cream and continue simmering and stirring until thickened. Put through blender until onions are liquefied. Return to soup pot to reheat, simmering and stirring until desired thickness. Add Tabasco, pour into heated tureen with absinthe and garnish with paprika. Serves 6. (Can be made in advance, refrigerated and reheated.)

CREAM OF CRAB SOUP

4 tablespoons butter
1 tablespoon minced onion
1 tablespoon minced celery
4 tablespoons flour
6 cups milk
2 cups cooked crabmeat (canned or frozen)
salt, pepper and Tabasco

Melt butter in a deep iron pot; add onion and celery, lightly sauté, and blend in flour. Gradually add scalded milk, stirring to keep smooth, then add crabmeat and season to taste. Cook in double boiler 15–20 minutes, or until well heated and thickened. May be served garnished with whipped cream and chopped parsley. Serves 6.

OYSTER SOUP

3 dozen oysters with liquid
2 tablespoons butter
1 tablespoon flour
2 tablespoons chopped green onions
1 pint half and half (milk and cream)
1 teaspoon butter
¼ teaspoon salt, or to taste
dash Tabasco

Heat oysters in liquid until their edges curl, then set aside to keep warm. Melt butter in a saucepan, blend in flour until smooth, stir in chopped green onions and simmer a few minutes. Put into a blender with oyster liquid and 1 dozen of the oysters. Blend first on low, then high for about a minute. While blending, add cream (at room temperature).

Melt 1 teaspoon butter in a double boiler, add soup and stir until well heated and thickened. Season soup. Add remaining oysters, or place 6 oysters in each warmed soup bowl and pour soup over them. Garnish with paprika. Serves 4. (Can be refrigerated and reheated.)

Gumbos

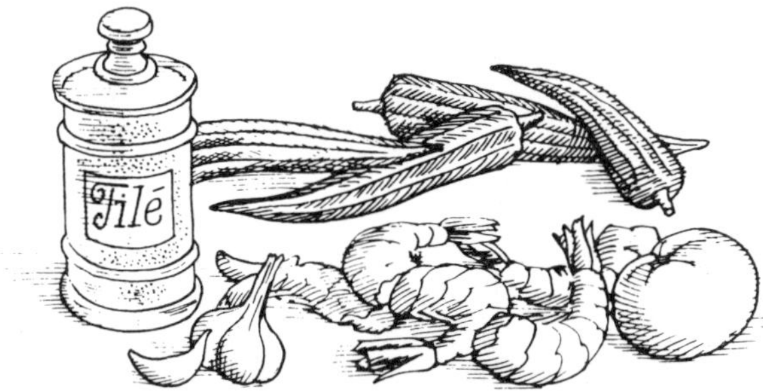

SEAFOOD GUMBO FILÉ

1 bunch green onions, chopped
2 tablespoons lard or bacon fat
3 tablespoons flour
1 sprig parsley, chopped
½ teaspoon thyme
1 rib celery, chopped
1 pint oyster liquid
2 pints water
1 pound raw shrimp, shelled
salt, pepper and Cayenne
2 dozen oysters
½ teaspoon gumbo filé powder

Sauté onions in fat in a deep iron pot. Stir in flour and add chopped parsley, thyme and celery. Cook a few minutes and add oyster liquid and water, shrimp and seasoning. Cover and cook slowly 1½ hours. Add oysters and cook until their edges curl. Remove from fire and stir in filé powder (gumbo should never be cooked after filé is added, so if you want to prepare in advance to reheat before serving, do so before adding filé). Serve in soup bowls with hot fluffy rice. Serves 6.

OKRA-SEAFOOD GUMBO

6 hardshell crabs
2 pounds okra
4 tablespoons bacon fat or lard
2 tablespoons flour
1 onion, chopped
2 green onions, chopped
1 pod garlic, chopped
1 green pepper, chopped
1 cup (¾ pound) cooked ham, diced
1 11-ounce can tomatoes
2 pounds raw shrimp
3 pints water
1 teaspoon salt, pinch of pepper
5 dashes Tabasco
1 bay leaf
¼ teaspoon thyme

Boil crabs until they turn red (about 20 minutes), set aside and reserve water in which they were boiled. Wash okra and cut into ¼-inch rounds. Put 2 tablespoons of fat in an iron skillet and fry okra, stirring often to prevent burning, until it is browned and dried out, with all trace of sliminess gone.

In a deep iron pot melt remaining 2 tablespoons of fat and blend in flour to make a roux, cooking and stirring until deep brown. Add chopped onion, garlic and green pepper, stir and cook a few minutes, then add ham. Add tomatoes and peeled raw shrimp. After cooking a few minutes, add cooked okra and 3 pints of crab-boiling water, or water. Add seasoning and let boil slowly about 2 hours, adding more water if necessary.

During this time, remove shell from crabs, crack claws with a nutcracker so they will pull apart easily, and either break bodies in half, or remove meat from them, depending on which way you prefer to serve them. During last half hour of cooking, add crab claws and halved bodies or meat to gumbo. (Although it is totally unconventional and certainly not as picturesque, if crabs are unavailable you will find that frozen Alaska King crab [½–1-pound package] can be used instead. It tastes good, and is not nearly as messy to eat or prepare.)

Gumbo is always served in a soup bowl over a teacup-molded mound of hot rice. This recipe, plus 1½ cups uncooked rice will serve 8 handsomely, and, with salad and French bread, makes a hearty meal. Will refrigerate and reheat well.

CHICKEN GUMBO

- 1 large stewing chicken, cut into serving pieces
- 6 tablespoons shortening
- 6 tablespoons flour
- 1 onion, minced
- ¼ cup diced celery
- 1 pod garlic, minced
- 6 cups hot water
- 1 tablespoon salt, or to taste
- 1 teaspoon black pepper, or to taste
- ½ cup chopped parsley
- ½–1 tablespoon gumbo filé powder

In a heavy pot, brown chicken in fat. After removing chicken, stir flour into fat to make a roux. Continue to cook, stirring constantly, until flour is dark brown, being careful not to burn. Add onion, celery and garlic, cooking until slightly wilted, then gradually add hot water, mixing to blend into roux. Add chicken, season, cover with tight-fitting lid and bring to steaming point. Lower heat and cook until chicken is tender, about 1–1½ hours, depending on size of chicken. Add parsley 5 minutes before removing from heat, then add filé powder. Do *not* cook after filé has been added. (If you must prepare in advance, do not add filé until just before serving.) Gumbo is always served in a soup plate over a teacup-molded mound of hot rice. This recipe, plus 1½ cups (uncooked) rice, serves 8.

Eggs

ABSINTHE BAKED EGGS

1 teaspoon butter
1 egg
1 tablespoon cream
1 teaspoon absinthe (Pernod)
dash Tabasco
pinch of salt,
  sprinkle of pepper
½ teaspoon grated Parmesan
  cheese (optional)

Preheat oven to 425° and melt butter in oven in shirred-egg dish or custard cup. Break egg into melted butter, add cream, Pernod, seasoning, and Parmesan, if you are using it, and bake at 425°, for 10 minutes for a soft yolk, or longer according to taste. Serves 1.

CREOLE OMELET

- 2 tablespoons bacon fat or cooking oil
- 1 medium onion, chopped
- 1 green pepper, chopped
- 1 pod garlic, chopped
- 1 11-ounce can tomatoes
- salt and pepper to taste
- 6 eggs
- 3 tablespoons butter

Melt fat in an iron skillet, sauté onion until transparent, add green pepper, garlic, tomatoes, salt and pepper, and simmer 15–20 minutes. Separate eggs. Beat whites until stiff, and fold into beaten yolks.

Melt butter in a large skillet and pour in eggs. When eggs have cooked a few minutes over a low flame, pour half of tomato sauce into center. Continue to cook slowly until eggs are cooked through to center, then transfer pan to broiler to cook and brown top. Serve on a platter with remaining tomato sauce poured over. Makes a delightful luncheon or supper dish with hot bread and salad. Serves 4.

EGGS SOUFFLÉ AU GRATIN

1 tablespoon butter
1 tablespoon flour
1 cup milk
salt, pepper and Cayenne

6 eggs
4 tablespoons grated
Cheddar cheese

Make a cream sauce by melting butter, stirring in flour and gradually adding milk. Cook, stirring until thickened, and season to taste. Pour half of this sauce into the bottom of a buttered baking dish.

Separate eggs, beat yolks lightly, beat whites until stiff, and fold yolks back into whites. Spread half of eggs in baking dish over layer of white sauce, sprinkle with half of grated cheese, pour in the remaining white sauce, cover with remaining egg, top with remaining cheese. Bake at 400° for 25–30 minutes, or until silver knife inserted in eggs comes out clean. Serves 3.

FISH SOUFFLÉ

1 small redfish (snapper)
salt, 1 pod hot red pepper
½ lemon, sliced
2 bay leaves
pinch of thyme
2 pods garlic
2 tablespoons butter
2 tablespoons flour
1 cup milk
2 tablespoons minced parsley
salt, pinch of Cayenne
2 teaspoons lemon juice
3 egg whites
bread crumbs

Put the fish in a deep pan and cover with water. Add salt, red pepper, lemon, bay leaves, thyme and garlic to the water, bring to a boil, and simmer until fish is cooked and will flake easily. Skin and flake fish.

Melt butter, stir in flour and blend in milk. Add parsley, salt and Cayenne, cook about 5 minutes, then add flaked fish. When well blended, take off fire and add lemon juice and seasoning to taste. Fold in stiffly beaten egg whites, put into a buttered casserole and sprinkle top with bread crumbs and a little melted butter. Put casserole into a pan of hot water and bake in 400° oven for 20–30 minutes and serve at once, with the following sauce. Serves 4–6.

SAUCE FOR FISH SOUFFLÉ

1 tablespoon butter
3 egg yolks
salt and Cayenne
1 tablespoon minced parsley
½ cup sherry

Melt butter in a double boiler, then add well-beaten egg yolks. Stir for a few minutes, then add salt and Cayenne to taste, and parsley. Continue stirring constantly until thickened and add sherry. Serve hot.

CRAB SOUFFLÉ

2 tablespoons butter
2 green onions, minced (white parts only)
2 tablespoons flour
1 small pod garlic, minced
1 cup light cream
1 pound cooked crabmeat (canned or frozen)
salt and Cayenne
3 egg whites

Melt butter, sauté onions and garlic lightly, and blend in flour. Gradually add cream, stirring constantly, then add crabmeat. Season to taste and fold in stiffly beaten egg whites. Pour into a buttered baking dish set in a pan of water, and bake at 400° for about 30 minutes. Serve immediately. Serves 4.

Seafood Specialties

OYSTERS WITH MUSHROOMS

¼ pound butter
1 onion, finely chopped
1 pod garlic, minced
½ cup finely chopped celery
1 heaping tablespoon flour
1 11-ounce can tomatoes, drained
salt, pepper and Cayenne
3 tablespoons Worcestershire sauce
1 medium can sliced mushrooms, drained
4 dozen oysters
bread crumbs

Melt butter. Sauté onion, garlic and celery until soft but not brown. Blend in flour and gradually stir in drained tomatoes. Mix well and add seasoning to taste and Worcestershire sauce, then mushrooms and drained oysters. Cook until edges of oysters curl. Put into an ovenproof serving dish, top with bread crumbs, dot with butter and bake in a moderate oven until very hot and bubbly. Serves 4–6.

OYSTERS IN RED WINE

4 tablespoons flour
¼ pound butter
1 medium onion, chopped
1 rib celery, chopped
1 tablespoon chopped parsley
5 dozen oysters
½ cup red wine
1 tablespoon parsley
½ cup mushrooms

Brown flour in butter in a deep skillet or heavy iron pot, cooking until very brown. Add onion, celery and parsley and simmer until transparent. Add oysters and cook until their edges curl, then remove these from sauce and set aside. Let sauce cook until very thick, then add wine. When well blended add oysters, parsley and mushrooms. Simmer until well heated and serve on toast points or rice. Serves 4.

OYSTER LOAF

2 dozen oysters
salt, pepper, Cayenne
1 cup milk
1 egg
bread crumbs
fat
2 small loaves French bread

Drain oysters and season. Dip in egg beaten into milk and roll in crumbs; repeat if desired for extra crispness. Fry breaded oysters in fat to cover until crisp and golden brown.

Split warmed loaves of French bread lengthwise and cut in half, making a sandwich with six oysters in each half. Serve with lemon wedges and pickles. Serves 2 or 4. Fine for lunch or supper, with cole slaw and French fries.

ARTICHOKES AND OYSTERS

6 artichokes
4½ dozen (or 2 pints) large oysters
4 tablespoons bacon fat or butter
4 tablespoons flour
4 tablespoons chopped green onions
½ bunch parsley, chopped
1 pod garlic, chopped
½ cup lemon juice
1 tablespoon Worcestershire sauce
scant ⅛ teaspoon Cayenne
½ teaspoon salt
½ teaspoon pepper
bread crumbs

Boil artichokes in salted water 30–45 minutes. Drain, chop hearts, and scrape tender part from leaves, reserving 4–6 whole leaves from each artichoke for garnish. (Discard scraped leaves.) Drain oysters, saving liquid. Heat oysters until edges curl, saving liquid residue in pan.

Make a roux in an iron pot with fat and flour, cooking until tan, not brown. Add onions, parsley and garlic, and after cooking a few minutes, add all liquid from oysters. When well blended, add artichoke and chopped oysters, lemon juice, Worcestershire sauce and seasoning.

Put into ramekins, sprinkle with crumbs, dot with butter and bake in a moderate oven until browned. Serve with artichoke leaves placed like petals around each ramekin. Serves 4 as entree or 6 as appetizer. Can be frozen before baking.

CREOLE STUFFED CABBAGE

1 large cabbage
½ cup bacon fat
1 bunch green onions, chopped
1 large rib celery, chopped
½ loaf French bread
3 dozen large oysters
¼ pound butter or margarine
salt and pepper

Hollow out a large head of cabbage, leaving about a 1-inch shell. Plunge the hollowed-out shell into a pot of boiling water. Let come to a boil again, remove cabbage, invert and drain. Shred the leaves cut from center of head, and boil until limp. Drain well.

Melt bacon fat in a skillet or iron pot, and fry green onions and celery. Add French bread, which has been broken up and moistened, or soaked in water and squeezed out. Fry with onions and celery until slightly brown. Drain oysters well, heat until edges curl, cut each in half and add to bread-onion dressing. Add cooked, shredded cabbage and a stick of butter or margarine and cook until butter melts. Season to taste.

Stuff this dressing loosely into cavity of cabbage head and

between remaining leaves. Put in a Dutch oven, adding ½–1 inch of water in bottom. Drizzle all over with a little bacon fat, cover tightly, bring to a boil and lower to simmer for 20–30 minutes. Remove cover and bake in 350° oven until brown, about 30 minutes, making sure there is always a little water in bottom. (Bake any leftover dressing in a separate casserole and serve around cabbage.) Serve cabbage by cutting into pie-shaped wedges.

Small cabbage rolls can be made in the same way by putting a big spoonful of the dressing into the center of a large (drained) cabbage leaf, folding ends in and rolling up. Place folded side down in a single layer in a baking dish, add water and bake. Serves 6–8.

CRABMEAT LAFAYETTE

¼ pound butter
3 medium onions, chopped
1 pod garlic, chopped
1 package frozen chopped spinach
½ small bunch parsley
leaves from 2 ribs celery
5 dashes Tabasco
1 teaspoon salt
¼ teaspoon pepper
1 teaspoon Worcestershire sauce
1 teaspoon absinthe (Pernod)
1½ pounds lump crabmeat
2 tablespoons butter
2 tablespoons flour
1½ cups milk
½ cup grated cheese

Sauté the chopped onions and garlic in butter until clear. Cook spinach and drain well. Put into a blender the parsley and celery leaves, and when they have been cut up, add spinach and onions, garlic and butter, and blend well. Add Tabasco, other seasoning and Pernod.

Make cheese sauce by melting the butter and blending in the flour. Then stir in milk, add grated cheese, and cook, stirring, until smooth and thickened.

Line individual ramekins with spinach mixture, cover with crabmeat, and top with cheese sauce. Bake in hot oven until browned on top. Serves 6. Can be prepared in advance and refrigerated before baking.

CRABMEAT WITH MUSHROOMS

2 tablespoons minced onion
1 tablespoon butter
1 tablespoon flour
1 cup cream
4 hardboiled egg yolks
salt, paprika
1 teaspoon lemon juice
1 cup cooked crabmeat (canned or frozen)
1 cup sliced mushrooms (canned or fresh)
bread crumbs

Sauté onion in butter until transparent, blend in flour, and gradually stir in cream. When sauce thickens, add mashed egg yolks, seasoning and lemon juice, then add crabmeat and mushrooms. (If fresh mushrooms are used, either blanch first in boiling water or sauté lightly in butter.) Cook a few minutes until well blended and thickened, then fill crab shells with mixture, or pour into individual ramekins. Cover with crumbs and dot with butter and brown in moderate oven. Serves 4.

STUFFED CRABS

- 2 tablespoons butter
- 3 green onions, chopped
- 1 tablespoon minced celery
- 1 tablespoon minced green pepper
- ½ pod garlic, minced
- 2 tablespoons minced parsley
- ½ loaf stale French bread
- ¼ teaspoon thyme
- 1 pound cooked crabmeat (canned or frozen)
- salt and Cayenne
- 1 egg
- bread crumbs

Melt butter in an iron skillet and sauté the onions, celery, green pepper, garlic and parsley. Break up stale bread, soak in water, squeeze out and add to ingredients in skillet. Sprinkle with thyme and fry until slightly browned; then add crabmeat and seasoning. Remove from fire and mix in egg.

Mound in well-cleaned crab shells or individual ramekins, cover with bread crumbs, dot with butter and bake in a moderate oven until browned. Garnish with lemon wedges and parsley sprigs. Serves 6.

SEAFOOD MARDI GRAS

2 tablespoons butter
2 tablespoons flour
2 cups milk
2 dozen oysters
1 pound shrimp, cooked, peeled and chopped
½ pound crabmeat
salt and Cayenne
½ cup grated cheese

Melt butter, stir in flour and blend in milk, stirring constantly until thickened. Drain oysters, heat in a dry skillet until edges curl, and add to cream sauce with chopped shrimp and crabmeat. Simmer until thick, season highly and pour into a baking dish or individual ramekins. Cover with grated cheese and bake in a moderate oven 15 minutes or until cheese is melted and slightly browned. Serves 4–6.

BROILED SHRIMP

24 raw shrimp
4 tablespoons butter
4 teaspoons lemon juice
8 dashes Tabasco
3 tablespoons bread crumbs
3 tablespoons grated Parmesan cheese

Peel and clean shrimp and pat dry. Put 1 tablespoon butter in each of 4 ramekins and melt in oven. Add 1 teaspoon lemon juice to each ramekin and lay 6 shrimp in each, not overlapping. Put a couple of dashes of Tabasco in each serving, and sprinkle with bread crumbs and Parmesan cheese. Put under broiler 7–10 minutes and serve at once. Serves 4 as appetizer; or divide into 2 or 3 larger baking dishes for entree.

SHRIMP AND CRAB FRICASSEE

- 8 hardshell crabs
- 1 pod hot red pepper
- 1 teaspoon salt
- 2 tablespoons butter
- 4 tablespoons flour
- 1 bunch green onions, chopped
- 1 rib celery, chopped
- 1 pod garlic, chopped
- 1 green pepper, chopped
- 2 bay leaves
- 4 cups water
- salt, Cayenne
- 2 pounds raw shrimp, peeled and cleaned
- 3 tablespoons sherry

Boil crabs in water with pod of red pepper and salt until they turn red (about 20 minutes). Reserve cooking water. Remove meat entirely from 4 crabs, including fat from top shells, and reserve. Remove hard top shells from remaining crabs, quarter crabs, and crack claws so they pull apart easily.

Melt butter in a deep iron pot. Stir in flour and continue cooking and stirring until roux is dark brown. Add onion, celery, garlic, green pepper and bay leaves. Add quartered crabs, cover and cook 5 minutes, stirring often. Add 2 cups of the water in which crabs were cooked, Cayenne and salt to taste, and let simmer 10 minutes. Add shrimp and 2 more cups crab water, and simmer ½ hour. Add reserved crabmeat, cook 5 minutes, stir in sherry and serve at once with rice. Serves 8–10.

COLD REDFISH MAYONNAISE

1 3-pound red snapper
salt and Cayenne
3 pods garlic
pinch thyme
1 bay leaf
1 sliced lemon
1 pod hot red pepper
½ teaspoon salt
½ cup homemade mayonnaise with 2 tablespoons whipped cream (optional)
Garnish: minced parsley, capers, lemon and olive slices, hardboiled eggs, tomatoes, asparagus, avocado slices, artichoke hearts

Wash the fish well, leaving head and tail on, and season well with salt and Cayenne. Put all ingredients through ½ teaspoon salt in a pan with enough water to cover fish, and boil a few minutes before adding fish. Poach fish in seasoned water for 10–15 minutes, or until done. Take fish from water and remove skin.

Snapper can either be refrigerated to serve whole, or meat can be removed from bones, molded together with a mixture of homemade mayonnaise and whipped cream (2 tablespoons whipped cream to ½ cup mayonnaise) and then refrigerated. In either case, garnish with minced parsley, capers, lemon and olive slices, and surround with hardboiled eggs, tomatoes, asparagus, avocado slices, artichoke hearts or any other cold vegetables. Serves 4–6.

If fish is served whole, the following tartar sauce may be served with it.

SAUCE TARTARE

- 2 teaspoons chopped capers
- 2 teaspoons chopped olives
- 2 teaspoons chopped parsley
- 2 teaspoons chopped pickles
- 2 green onions, chopped
- ½ cup mayonnaise

Combine ingredients just before serving. Makes about 1 cup.

Rice Dishes

CREOLE JAMBALAYA

1 onion, chopped
2 tablespoons chopped green onion
1 pod garlic, minced
1 teaspoon minced parsley
½ teaspoon thyme
2 tablespoons lard or bacon fat
1 pound cubed cooked ham
½ pound chaurice (Chorizo) or any hot spiced small sausage
2 cups water
1 cup uncooked rice
salt and pepper
½ pound cooked shrimp, cleaned and shelled
1 dozen oysters

Sauté onions, garlic, parsley and thyme in fat in a large iron pot. Add ham and skinned sausage, cook a few minutes, then add water and bring to a boil. Add washed rice and seasoning to taste. Simmer, covered, until rice is done and nearly dry (about 30 minutes), adding more water if needed to complete cooking of rice. Heat oysters in their liquid until edges curl. During last 5 minutes of cooking the jambalaya add shrimp, and oysters with their liquid. Serves 6–8.

HAM JAMBALAYA

1 cup rice
4 tablespoons bacon fat or shortening
1 large onion, chopped
1 cup cooked ham, cubed
1 green pepper, chopped
1 pod garlic
1 11-ounce can tomatoes
1 cup water
½ teaspoon thyme
1 bay leaf
salt, pepper and Tabasco
1 cup peeled raw shrimp (optional)

Wash rice in a strainer until clear, and then fry with fat and onion in a large deep skillet or heavy iron pot. When rice is golden brown, add ham, green pepper and garlic, then tomatoes, water and all seasoning.

Cook slowly until rice has absorbed liquid and is tender—about 30–35 minutes. If shrimp is being used, add after 10 or 15 minutes of cooking. Crab, oysters, chicken or almost anything can also be added: the word jambalaya is said to mean "clean up the kitchen." Makes a fine meal with salad and corn bread. Serves 6.

HOPPING JOHN

2 cups (1 pound) dried black-eyed peas
3 pints cold water
½ pound salt pork or bacon cut in thirds
1 teaspoon Tabasco
½ teaspoon salt
1 small bay leaf
dash garlic powder
2 medium onions, chopped
2 tablespoons bacon fat or lard
1 cup uncooked rice

Cover peas with water and soak overnight. Add salt pork or bacon, Tabasco, salt, bay leaf and garlic powder, and simmer about 1 hour.

Meanwhile sauté onions in fat until yellow, and add to peas with rice and additional boiling water if necessary. Cook until rice is tender and water absorbed, about 20–25 minutes, stirring occasionally. Taste for seasoning and add more salt and pepper if desired. Serves 8.

RED BEANS AND RICE I

Typical Louisiana poor folk's food, the South's equivalent of Italian spaghetti dishes, and just as good.

2 cups (1 pound) dried red kidney beans
2½ quarts water
5 strips bacon (or a ham bone or ¼ pound salt pork)
1 pod garlic
salt and pepper to taste
½ cups (uncooked) rice

Soak beans overnight in 1 quart water in a heavy iron pot. Add another 1½ quarts water, cut-up bacon (or a ham bone or salt pork), garlic and a little salt, and simmer slowly 3–4 hours, or until beans are very soft and water has cooked down to a thick red sauce. Add salt and pepper to taste, and serve over hot fluffy rice (cooked by whatever method you prefer). With hot bread and salad makes a hearty meal for 6.

Leftover red beans can be made into soup by putting through blender with some chicken bouillon and a little lemon juice. Stir in 1 tablespoon of sherry per serving, with grated hardboiled egg sprinkled on top.

RED BEANS AND RICE II

2 cups dried red kidney beans
2½ quarts water
3 tablespoons shortening or bacon fat
1 large onion, chopped
1 small green pepper, chopped
¼ pound salt pork (or a ham bone)
1 pod garlic
1 bay leaf
salt and pepper to taste
2 tablespoons chopped parsley
1½ cups (uncooked) rice

Soak beans in water overnight. Melt fat in an iron pot and sauté onion and green pepper. Add beans, soaking water plus enough additional water to make 2½ quarts, pork (or ham bone), garlic and bay leaf, and simmer slowly 3–4 hours or until creamy. Season to taste, add parsley; serve over hot cooked rice. Serves 6.

SHRIMP CREOLE

- 2 pounds raw shrimp
- 4 tablespoons bacon fat or shortening
- 4 tablespoons flour
- 1 small onion, chopped
- 1 11-ounce can tomatoes
- 2 cups water
- 1 pod garlic, chopped
- ½ teaspoon thyme
- 1 bay leaf
- 1 tablespoon chopped green pepper
- 3 tablespoons chopped celery
- salt and pepper to taste
- 1½ cups (uncooked) rice

Peel, devein and wash shrimp. Make a roux with fat, flour and onion. When slightly browned, stir in tomatoes and simmer a few minutes, then add water, shrimp and all seasonings. Simmer about a half hour, pour over hot cooked rice and serve. Refrigerates and reheats well. Serves 6.

GRILLADES

- 2 pounds veal round or scaloppine
- 4 tablespoons bacon fat or lard
- 4 tablespoons flour
- 1 medium onion, chopped
- 1 11-ounce can tomatoes
- 1½ cups water
- 1 green pepper, chopped
- 1 pod garlic, chopped
- ½ teaspoon thyme
- 1 bay leaf
- 1 tablespoon chopped parsley
- salt, pepper and Tabasco
- 1½ cups (uncooked) rice

Cut veal into serving pieces and fry in shortening in a deep iron pot until well browned. Remove veal and make a roux with the fat remaining in pan, the flour and onions. Brown well, then add tomatoes. After simmering a few minutes, add water, meat and all other ingredients. Simmer slowly for about an hour until veal is very tender, adding water if necessary to make sauce the consistency of thick gravy. It is customary to serve grillades (which can also be made with beef) over rice. This recipe, with the cooked rice, corn bread and salad, should serve 6. Can be refrigerated and reheated.

CHICKEN FRICASSEE POINTE COUPÉE

- 3–4-pound young chicken, cut up
- 2 tablespoons butter
- 2 tablespoons flour
- 2 cups warm water
- 2 tablespoons chopped parsley
- ½ teaspoon thyme
- 1 bay leaf
- 2 tablespoons lemon juice
- 1 teaspoon salt
- ¼ teaspoon pepper
- dash Cayenne
- 10 small whole white onions
- ½ cup mushrooms (canned or fresh)
- 1 egg yolk
- 1 cup (uncooked) rice

Soak chicken in water with a tablespoon of vinegar for 1 hour to whiten and make tender. Pat dry with paper toweling. In a large iron pot, melt butter, stir in flour and gradually add water, stirring constantly. Add herbs, lemon juice and seasoning, then chicken. After simmering a few minutes add onions; and about ½ hour before serving add mushrooms (if fresh mushrooms are used, blanch them first in boiling water). When chicken is cooked (about 1 hour), remove from sauce. Thicken sauce with a liaison made by taking 3 tablespoons of sauce and beating well with egg yolk. Take remaining sauce from fire and blend in egg mixture. Return chicken to sauce and serve with cooked rice or noodles. Serves 4. Tastes delightfully interesting and different served cold.

CREOLE COURTBOUILLON

- 1 tablespoon lard or bacon fat
- 6 onions, chopped
- 2 tablespoons flour
- 1 pod garlic, minced
- 1 tablespoon minced parsley
- 2 ribs celery, chopped
- 1 bay leaf
- pinch of thyme
- 2 11-ounce cans tomatoes
- 1 pint water
- salt, pepper and Cayenne
- 4 pounds redfish (snapper), sliced
- 1 lemon, sliced
- 1½ cups (uncooked) rice

Melt fat in deep kettle and fry onions until golden. Stir in flour, then garlic, parsley, celery, bay leaf and thyme. Cook a few minutes, stirring, then add tomatoes and water. Bring to a boil, add salt, pepper and Cayenne and boil 5 minutes more. Add fish and lemon and simmer for ½ hour.

Remove fish to a hot platter, discard bay leaf and boil sauce well, stirring, for a few minutes. Pour over fish and serve with cooked rice. Serves 8–10.

Vegetables

CREOLE STRING BEANS

2 pounds string beans
3 pints water
¼ pound salt pork
salt and pepper

Prepare beans for cooking, breaking each into 2 or 3 pieces, and cook slowly in water with salt pork about 2 hours. Season to taste, cook 30 minutes longer, drain well and serve. Serves 4–6.

STEWED OKRA AND TOMATOES

1 pound okra
4 tablespoons bacon fat
2 green peppers, chopped
½ cup chopped onions
1 11-ounce can tomatoes
1 garlic pod, pressed
1 teaspoon lemon juice
1 teaspoon salt

Slice okra in ⅛-inch rounds, discarding ends. Cook in fat in heavy pot, stirring constantly to prevent burning, until sliminess disappears. Add green peppers and onions and cook until transparent. Add tomatoes, garlic, lemon juice, and salt to taste. Simmer about 15 minutes.

Can be served with cooked chopped ham or shrimp added 5 minutes before serving. Serves 4.

LETTUCE AU JUS

2 small heads iceberg lettuce
2 tablespoons butter
1 tablespoon flour
1 cup chicken stock
1 teaspoon minced celery
1 teaspoon minced parsley
½ bay leaf
pinch thyme
¼ teaspoon salt
⅛ teaspoon pepper

Remove loose outside leaves of lettuce. Clean and cook quartered heads 10–20 minutes in boiling water. Remove, dip in cold water, and drain. Melt butter, stir in flour, browning a little. Add stock, herbs and seasonings and lettuce, and simmer ½ hour, basting often. Serves 4–8.

BAKED CABBAGE AU GRATIN

1 small cabbage
2 tablespoons butter
2 tablespoons flour
1½ cups milk
2 tablespoons grated Cheddar cheese
salt and pepper
celery salt
1 tablespoon chopped parsley
bread crumbs

Cut cabbage in quarters and boil in salted water until tender. Drain and place in baking dish. Melt butter, stir in flour, gradually add milk, stirring until thickened. Add half of grated cheese and seasoning to taste. Pour over cabbage, sprinkle with chopped parsley and bread crumbs and remaining cheese and bake in a moderate oven until brown. Serves 4.

BAKED CELERY

1 large bunch celery
1 tablespoon butter
1 tablespoon flour
1 cup milk
3 tablespoons grated American cheese
¾ teaspoon salt
¼ teaspoon pepper
2 dashes Tabasco
buttered bread crumbs

Cut celery in serving pieces and boil in lightly salted water until soft, about 25–30 minutes. Drain celery and keep warm. Make a white sauce by melting butter, blending in flour and gradually adding milk. When thickened, add grated cheese and seasoning, and pour over celery in a shallow ovenproof serving dish. Cover top with buttered bread crumbs and bake at 425° until golden brown. Serves 4–6.

SPINACH AND ASPARAGUS

- 1 package frozen chopped spinach
- 1 large can white asparagus
- 2 tablespoons butter
- 2 tablespoons flour
- 1½ cups milk
- salt and pepper
- bread crumbs

Cook spinach according to directions on package and drain very well. Arrange drained asparagus in the bottom of a wide, shallow baking dish in a single layer covering bottom of dish.

Make a cream sauce by melting butter in a saucepan, blending in flour and gradually adding milk. Stir until thickened and season to taste. Pour a few tablespoons of cream sauce around asparagus in baking dish and mix remainder into drained spinach, tasting again for seasoning.

Cover the asparagus with the creamed spinach, and cover the top with bread crumbs. Bake in a moderate oven until thoroughly heated and browned on top. Serves 6. (Can be refrigerated until ready for baking.)

FRIED EGGPLANT

1 large eggplant
1½ cups milk
1 teaspoon salt
½ teaspoon sugar
1 egg
cornmeal or cracker meal
vegetable oil for frying

Peel whole eggplant, slice in half and cut into wedges full length of eggplant and about 1 inch thick. Cut off as many seeds as possible. Put wedges into a bowl, cover with milk, salt and sugar, and marinate in refrigerator 4–5 hours. When ready to cook, dip wedges in beaten egg and roll in fine cornmeal or cracker meal.

Heat oil in a skillet at least 1½ inches deep and fry wedges until crisp and golden brown. Drain on absorbent paper and keep warm in oven until all are fried and ready to serve. Can be used as a vegetable or as an appetizer with cocktails. Serves 4–6, depending on size of eggplant.

STUFFED EGGPLANT

2 eggplants
2 tablespoons fat
1 tablespoon butter
2 onions, chopped
3 tablespoons bread crumbs
1 cup chopped cooked ham
salt and pepper

Boil eggplants for 20 minutes and let cool. Cut in half lengthwise and scoop out centers, keeping shell intact. Melt fat and butter in a skillet and sauté onions. Add eggplant meat, bread crumbs and ham, stir and fry a few minutes. Season, then stuff into eggplant shells. Sprinkle with additional crumbs and bake at 350° for about 30 minutes. Serves 4–8.

STUFFED PEPPERS

6 large green peppers
1½ pounds raw, shelled shrimp, fresh or frozen
1 bunch green onions, chopped
2 ribs celery, chopped
4 tablespoons bacon fat, butter or margarine
1 small loaf French bread
2 tablespoons chopped parsley
salt, pepper, dash Tabasco

Parboil halved and seeded green peppers in salted water for 20–25 minutes, or until they change color. Drop shrimp in boiling water and cook 5–10 minutes, or until they turn pink. Peel, chop and set aside.

Sauté the onions and celery in fat until transparent. Break French bread into a bowl of water. Soak for a few minutes, then squeeze out and add to fried onions and celery. Cook, stirring, until bread is dried out and slightly browned. Add shrimp, parsley and seasoning, and cook a few minutes, mixing well.

Stuff into halved peppers in shallow baking dish. Add ½ inch of water around peppers to prevent drying out, and dot tops with butter. Bake at 350° about 45 minutes. Ham or bacon may be substituted for, or added to, shrimp. Serves 6–12, depending on what is served with it.

JULIUS CAESAR TOMATOES

Delightfully different and particularly good in hot weather.

6 tomatoes
4 hardboiled eggs
8 stuffed olives
8 anchovy filets
4 tablespoons chopped celery
2 teaspoons capers
2 tablespoons mayonnaise
6 anchovy filets for garnish

Scoop out tomatoes. Finely chop eggs, olives, anchovies, celery and capers, and mix together with mayonnaise. Stuff tomatoes with this mixture and freeze until almost hard before serving. Or store in freezer and remove to thaw at room temperature about ½ hour before serving. Serve on a bed of lettuce topped with a dab of mayonnaise and garnished with an anchovy. Serves 6.

Accompaniments

CONFEDERATE PUDDING
(Baked Grits)

1 cup milk
1 cup water
½ teaspoon salt
1 cup grits

½ cup milk
1 tablespoon butter
2 eggs, separated

Put 1 cup milk and water together in a pot with salt and bring to a boil. Slowly sprinkle in the grits, stirring constantly. Turn down fire and cook very slowly, stirring until thick. Add ½ cup milk and the butter, continuing to stir. Remove from fire and stir in egg yolks. Fold in stiffly beaten egg whites, and bake in buttered dish at 350° about 30 minutes. Serve with hash or stew, or as an alternative to potatoes, rice or noodles. Serves 4.

CORN BREAD DRESSING

Can be served in a casserole with Oyster-Mushroom Gravy, or as a stuffing for turkey, chicken or individual chicken breasts, or served with any hot meat (such as roast beef) with its gravy.

½ stick butter
1 heaping tablespoon finely chopped green onions
3 tablespoons finely chopped parsley
3 cups corn bread crumbs
3 cups toasted white or French bread crumbs
salt and pepper
1 egg, beaten
1½ cups water

Melt butter in an iron skillet and sauté onions and parsley until they are just limp, not brown. Add crumbs and seasoning to taste. Add beaten egg and water, mix well and place in greased 1½-2 quart casserole (or stuff in turkey). Dot with butter and bake at 350° for about 35 minutes, or until browned. Serve with Oyster-Mushroom Gravy. Serves 6.

OYSTER-MUSHROOM GRAVY

½ stick butter
3 tablespoons flour
2 heaping tablespoons finely chopped green onions
2 cups chicken stock or water
2 tablespoons white wine
salt and pepper
2 3-ounce cans sliced mushrooms browned in butter
3–4 dozen oysters
1 tablespoon chopped parsley

Melt butter in an iron skillet and blend in flour to make a roux, cooking until it becomes a rich brown. Add onions, and after cooking a few minutes, add stock, wine and liquid drained from mushrooms. Cook down until very thick. Season lightly, allowing for saltiness of oysters, bring to a boil and add well-drained mushrooms and oysters. After bringing to a boil again, simmer slowly 15 minutes. Serve sprinkled with fresh chopped parsley, in a gravy boat. Serves 6.

FRIED GRITS

- 2½ cups water
- ½ teaspoon salt
- ½ cup grits
- 2 eggs
- salt and pepper
- flour or cracker crumbs
- fat

This is usually made with leftover grits, but to start from scratch, boil salted water, gradually add grits, stirring to keep from forming lumps, then simmer slowly for 25–30 minutes, stirring occasionally. Pour into a shallow pan or dish large enough so that grits are only about 1 inch deep. Refrigerate overnight or at least until grits are cold and firm.

Slice into 3–4-inch pieces and dip into seasoned beaten egg, roll in flour and repeat. Fry in ½ inch of fat until crisp golden brown, and drain on absorbent paper. This is excellent served with dinner instead of rice or potatoes, but it can also be eaten with syrup for breakfast. Serves 4.

SWEET POTATO BALLS

6 medium-size sweet potatoes
  or yams
1 cup sugar
1 teaspoon salt
1 cup chopped pecans
2 cups crushed
  corn flakes
fat for frying

Boil potatoes, peel, mash, mix in sugar and salt, and chill for 2 hours. Add pecans, roll into walnut-size balls, roll in crushed corn flakes until well coated, and fry immediately in hot fat until crisp and brown. It is important to fry at once without too much handling, or potato balls will become too soft to keep their shape. Serves 8.

Sweets

FROZEN BUTTERMILK

This unique dessert has the delightful tart-sweet flavor of the Frozen Cream Cheese made only in the vicinity of New Orleans where Creole cream cheese is available.

1 quart buttermilk
1 pint heavy cream
pinch of soda
1 cup sugar
2 teaspoons vanilla
4 egg whites

Mix together all ingredients except egg whites. Beat egg whites until very stiff in electric mixer, then add other ingredients and beat together. Freeze, stirring occasionally to prevent separation. Tastes best if served when still light and creamy, before it freezes hard. Serves 10–12, or quantities can easily be cut in half to serve 6.

BRANDY CUSTARD

4 egg yolks
1 teaspoon vanilla
1 teaspoon sugar
½ pint whipping cream
4 tablespoons dark-brown sugar
4 teaspoons French brandy

Put egg yolks in blender and blend until light and foamy. Add vanilla, sugar and cream, and blend 30 seconds. Into each of 4 custard cups put 1 tablespoon brown sugar and 1 teaspoon brandy. Slowly pour custard into cups and place cups in a baking pan. Pour water into pan until it reaches halfway up the cups, and bake at 350° for 45–60 minutes, until tops are golden brown with cracks running through. Eat hot, or refrigerate to serve cold. Serves 4.

RUM BANANAS

3 bananas
1 tablespoon lemon juice
3 tablespoons brown sugar
1 tablespoon butter
1½–2 tablespoons rum

Wash bananas and cut them in half lengthwise. Do not peel. Lay them in a baking pan with the cut side facing up and sprinkle with lemon juice and brown sugar and dot with butter. Let sit for ½ hour, pour rum over them and put under broiler for 10–15 minutes. Baste once or twice, and serve when bubbling hot. Serves 3–6. This recipe may also be used to broil grapefruit.

PLUM-PECAN CONSERVE

6 pounds blue Italian plums
4 pounds sugar
1 orange rind, grated
juice of 3 oranges
juice of 2 lemons
2 pounds seedless raisins
1 pound pecans

Remove seeds from plums and cook plums with sugar, grated rind and juices for about 1½ hours. Add raisins during last ½ hour, and add pecans while cooling. Makes about 2 quarts. Freezes well. Serve with fowl or meat, or for dessert.

PRALINES

This is so quick and easy that it should almost be called "Instant Pralines."

1 cup syrup, maple or golden
3 cups sugar
pinch of salt
2 cups shelled pecan halves

Cook syrup, sugar and salt together in an aluminum pot. When mixture comes to a boil, stir in pecans. Stir constantly for about 5–10 minutes, or until mixture thickens. Drop by spoonfuls on a sheet of waxed paper. (If you want to be sure it has reached the right consistency, test by dropping a small amount on paper first: if it begins to harden immediately, it is ready; if not, cook a little longer. Cooking too long results in grainy, sugary texture.) When pralines cool and harden they will peel off easily. Makes about 2 dozen large pralines.

Filé
1962
Graves
BORDEAUX